ROUGH, TOUGH *Charley*

by **VERLA KAY**

Illustrated by **ADAM GUSTAVSON**

TRICYCLE PRESS
BERKELEY / TORONTO

Charley, orphan,
Runs from town.
Hides in stable,
Hunkers down.

Found by owner.
Horses neigh.
"You can't sleep there,
In my hay!"

Charley cowers,
Hangs his head.
"Druther sleep here,
Than in bed."

Then he stands up,
"That there mare
Gots a problem—
Matted hair."

"N'yonder horse jest
Threw a shoe."
Charley begging,
"Work fer you?"

Owner ponders,
Nods his head.
"I need help.
You need a bed."

Charley working,
Handles reins.
Learns to doctor
Cuts and sprains.

Charley driving!
Gaining fame.
Folks requesting
Him by name.

CALIFORNIA STAGE CO.

DRYTOWN AND JACKSON.

Daylor's Rancho, Wilson's Exchange, Mountain House, Dry
Town, Sutter Creek, Willow Springs, White Cottage,
Amador, Arkansas.

Greenwood Valley and Georgetown

Town, Greenwood Valley, Knickerbocker Rancho, Mur-
Centreville, Pilot Hill, Indian Springs, Salmon
Willow Springs, Lexington House
Alder Creek.
Snake Bar,

Drivers needed,
Way out west.
Steamship carries
Charley, chest.

Six-horse stagecoach
Bounds along.
Charley reins up,
Flicks a thong.

Ladies gossip,
"Charley's odd.
Don't like people."
Then they nod.

"And he's vulgar.
Chews and spits.
Gambles, swears, and
Even hits."

"But he's always
  Smack on time.
  Stops his stagecoach
  On a dime!"

"Charley don't have
  Accidents.
  Springs those horses.
  He's got sense!"

"That's our Charley,
  He's the best,
  Even though he's
  Fancy-dressed."

Bandit! Hold up!
Bullets shoot!
Bad man buried.
"Saved the loot."

Bumping, bouncing,
Cloppety clip.
Dusty, dirty,
Cracking whip.

"Them's me beauties,
They go fast.
How I loves 'em—
DRAT IT! BLAST!"

"Jumpy horse just
Kicked me eye!"
(Charley's tough though,
He don't cry.)

Stagecoach slowing,
Steep slope, slide!
Jostles people,
Side to side.

One-eyed Charley,
Driving still.
Safely down and
Up each hill.

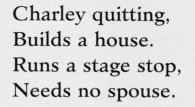

Charley quitting,
Builds a house.
Runs a stage stop,
Needs no spouse.

Charley votes for
Presidents.
Joins a lodge with
Other gents.

Charley ailing,
Can't eat bread.
Nursing sore throat,
Sick in bed.

People ask him,
"Should we go?
Get the doctor?"
Charley, "NO!"

Charley's deathbed,
Faces grim.
Local doctor,
"Bury him."

Hold your horses!
Huge surprise . . .

"*He's a woman,*
 In disguise!"

Women were not
"Rough and tough."
They weren't "smart
Or strong enough."

They were bound by
Petticoats.
Couldn't drive or
Cast their votes.

Charley did though—
As she would.
Drove and voted,
Cause "he" could.

FACTS ABOUT CHARLEY

Charley Darkey, or Durkey, Parkhurst, was born in 1812 in New Hampshire. **1** As a youth, she ran away from an orphanage located somewhere in Massachusetts.

Ebenezer Balch ran a livery stable in Worcester, Massachusetts. **2** Charley was first discovered hiding with the horses. She worked for Ebenezer for many years and moved with him to the *What Cheer* stables in Providence, Rhode Island, **3** in the early 1840s.

Charley had blue-grey eyes, stood 5' 7" tall, and rarely was seen without a wide belt, box-pleated blousy shirts, and fancy embroidered gloves.

Shortly after a heavy storm, a bridge began breaking up while Charley's stagecoach crossed the Tuolumne River near Modesto, California. **5** Charley saved the passengers by springing the horses forward, bringing the stagecoach onto solid ground just as the bridge collapsed into the river.

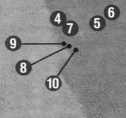

In the early 1850s, Charley shot a notorious bandit on Mukulomne Hill in Calaveras County, California, **6** during an attempted stage robbery. The bandit was called Sugarfoot because he wore sugar sacks on his feet—supposedly to avoid leaving tracks during his escape.

On April 25, 1867, "Charley Durkey Parkhurst, age 55, native of New Hampshire, farmer by occupation, currently residing in Soquel" registered to vote. She voted at the Soquel Firehouse on November 3, 1868, one year before the state of Wyoming allowed women to vote, and fifty-two years before the federal government gave all women the right to vote.

On December 28, 1879, Charley died of cancer of the tongue. She had always doctored herself with the same remedies she used on her horses. Her belief: "If it's good enough fer me horses, it's good enough fer me."

Charley's true sex was discovered and documented by Dr. Lambert Irelan.

On December 17, 1852, Pacific Mail steamship *The Golden Gate* landed in San Francisco, California, **④** carrying 460 passengers, including one Charles O. Parkhurst.

Charley worked for the California Stage Company, Wells Fargo, and Dillon, Hedge & Company driving various routes from Virginia City, Nevada, to San Juan Bautista, California.

Charley was noted as one of the safest and fastest drivers in the Motherlode. Her stagecoaches were always on time and none of her passengers were ever injured.

In 1859, Charley retired to Soquel, California, **⑧** built a cabin, worked in the local lumber mills, and raised cattle with a partner named Frank Woodward. It was said that when Frank discovered Charley was a woman, he was so upset he "didn't stop swearing for three days!"

Charley's left eye was kicked out by a horse in Redwood City, California, **⑦** in 1856 while replacing a horseshoe on the San Francisco to San Jose run.

Charley ran a stage stop called "Sand House Station" located at the old Seven Mile House at 4197 Freedom Boulevard near Aptos, California. **⑨**

On October 18, 1867, Charley joined the Soquel Chapter (Lodge 137) of the International Order of Odd Fellows. Charley was the first woman known to have joined the club and she held continuous membership until her death. She was buried with full lodge honors because her lodge brothers respected her so much as a "man."

On December 28, 1879, Charley was buried in the local Odd Fellows (Pioneer) cemetery in Watsonville, California. **⑩**

Charley left all her worldly goods (about $600) to George Harmon, the 14-year-old neighbor boy she befriended during her final days.

On January 3, 1880, the *Santa Cruz Sentinel* printed an obituary of Charley Parkhurst that ended with the statement:

"Who shall longer say that a woman can not labor and vote like a man?"

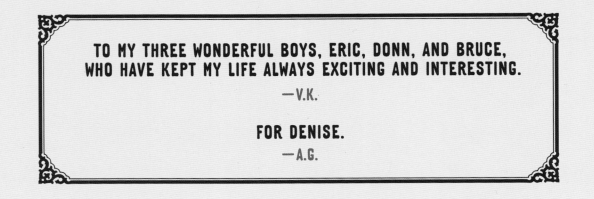

TO MY THREE WONDERFUL BOYS, ERIC, DONN, AND BRUCE,
WHO HAVE KEPT MY LIFE ALWAYS EXCITING AND INTERESTING.
—V.K.

FOR DENISE.
—A.G.

Tricycle Press
an imprint of Ten Speed Press
PO Box 7123
Berkeley, California 94707
www.tricyclepress.com

Design by Barbara Grzeslo and Betsy Stromberg
Typeset in Minister
The illustrations in this book were rendered in oils.

Photograph of headstone from Pioneer Cemetery in Watsonville,
California, courtesy Pajaro Valley Historical Association.

Library of Congress Cataloging-in-Publication Data

Kay, Verla.
  Rough, tough Charley / by Verla Kay ; illustrated by Adam
Gustavson.
     p. cm.
  ISBN-13: 978-1-58246-184-7
  ISBN-10: 1-58246-184-8
  1. Parkhurst, Charley, d. 1879--Juvenile literature. 2. Women
pioneers--California--Biography--Juvenile literature. 3.
Pioneers--California--Biography--Juvenile literature. 4. Coach
drivers--California--Biography--Juvenile literature. 5. Mistaken
identity--California--Juvenile literature. 6.
California--History--1850-1950--Juvenile literature. I. Gustavson,
Adam,
ill. II. Title.
  F864.P27K395 2007
  979.4'04092--dc22
  [B]
                                              2006026611

First Tricycle Press printing, 2007
Printed in China

1 2 3 4 5 6 — 11 10 09 08 07